OIL'S QUEST

By Cody Nernberg

Illustrated By David Bou

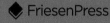 FriesenPress

Suite 300 - 990 Fort St
Victoria, BC, V8V 3K2
Canada

www.friesenpress.com

ISBN
978-1-5255-8500-5 (Hardcover)
978-1-5255-8499-2 (Paperback)
978-1-5255-8501-2 (eBook)

1. JUVENILE NONFICTION, SCIENCE & NATURE, EARTH SCIENCES, GEOGRAPHY

Distributed to the trade by The Ingram Book Company

Printed in Canada

DEDICATED TO KADEN AND KAI.

You inspire me daily.
Never stop dreaming.

ATTENTION FRIENDS!

Look for these items when you read this book.

Can you spot them all?

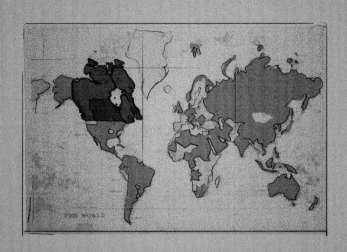

MAP

PUMP JACK

TRAIN

CANADIAN FLAG

Oil is formed. Oil is formed.

OCEAN
300 to 400 MILLION YEARS AGO

PLANTS AND ANIMALS

OCE
50 to 100 MILL

SAND A
PLANT AND A

4

TIME. PRESSURE. UNSEEN.

AN
ON YEARS AGO

D SILT

MAL REMAINS

TODAY

SAND AND SILT

TRAPPED OIL

Look for oil. Look for oil.

UNDERGROUND. LAND. MARINE.

Oil was found. Oil was found.

GEOPHONES (VIBRATION DETECTORS)

8

RESERVOIR. DEPOSIT. ONSHORE.

SEISMIC WAVES
(SHOCK WAVES)

Drill the well. **Drill** the well.

10

DEEP. FORMATION. EXPLORE.

Extract the oil. Extract the oil.

12

LIFT. PUMP. MAINTAIN.

Separate the oil. Separate the oil.

Move the oil. Move the oil.

RAIL. TRUCK. PIPELINE.

Store the oil. Store the oil.

OIL

COLLECT. SECURE. CONFINE.

Distill the oil. Distill the oil.

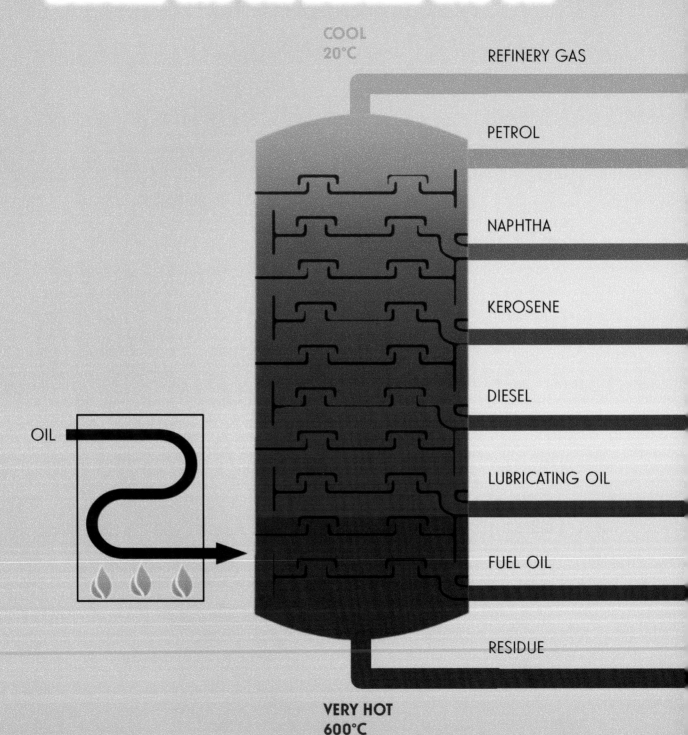

COOL
20°C

REFINERY GAS

PETROL

NAPHTHA

KEROSENE

DIESEL

LUBRICATING OIL

FUEL OIL

RESIDUE

OIL

VERY HOT
600°C

DIESEL. KEROSENE. GASOLINE.

BOTTLED GAS

GASOLINE

CHEMICALS

JET FUEL

DIESEL FUEL

LUBRICATING OILS

FUEL FOR SHIPS

BITUMEN FOR ROADS

Refine it further. Refine it further.

BLEND. TREAT. CLEAN.

Oil makes more. **Oil** makes more.

24

TABLETS. PHONES. LAPTOPS.

SUNGLASSES. POLYESTER. FLIP-FLOPS.

Sell it globally. Sell it globally.

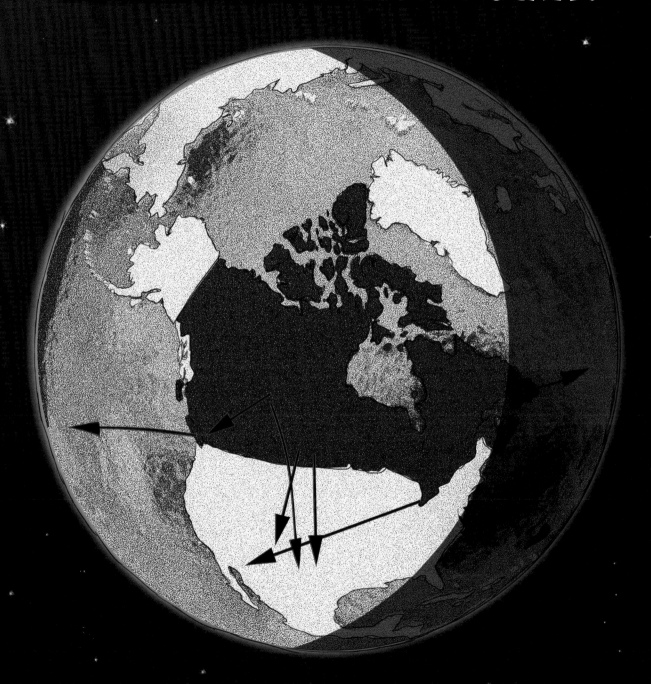

Job is done. **Job** is done.

CANADIAN. PROUD. CELEBRATE.

FREQUENTLY ASKED QUESTIONS

💧 ## What is **oil**?

Oil, also known as crude oil or petroleum, is a naturally occurring yellowish-black liquid that is trapped in underground rock all over the world.

💧 ## How is **oil** formed?

Millions of years ago, marine mammals and vegetation died and settled on the bottoms of oceans, seas, lakes, and rivers forming layers of organic material. Over thousands of years, rock and sand covered these layers applying pressure. Over time, heat from the earth's interior cooked the organic material and changed it into the oil we extract from the ground today.

How is **oil** found?

The most commonly used method for locating oil is called seismology, where shock waves are created that pass through hidden rock and layers underground. The waves are reflected back by various rock layers at different speeds. Sensitive microphones or vibration detectors detect the reflections of the shock waves. The readings are interpreted for signs of oil deposits.

How many products are made from **oil**?

Over 6,000 products get their start from oil including children's toys, computers, golf balls, skis, snowboards, toothpaste, and makeup.

GLOSSARY

ADVERTISE: Also known as advertising, refers to making your product or service known to an audience through paid announcements in mediums such as magazines, websites, radio, and television.

DEPOSIT: An area underground where a large amount of oil is found.

DIESEL: A liquid that is made from oil and used as fuel for trucks, trains, school buses, farm, and construction equipment.

DISTILL: The process of heating oil and passing it through a vessel to separate out different compounds, known as fractions.

EXTRACT: The process by which oil is drawn out from beneath the earth's surface location.

FORMATION: An underground layer that is made up of the same kind of rock or rock types.

GASOLINE: A liquid that is made from oil and used as fuel for cars, sport utility vehicles, and light trucks.

KEROSENE: A liquid that is made from oil and is widely used in jet fuel for airplanes as well as a cooking and lighting fuel.

MARINE: Of the ocean or sea.

MARKET: Also known as marketing, refers to preparing a product to be sold.

ONSHORE: Situated or occurring on land.

POLYESTER: Fiber made from oil that is used for making a wide variety of clothing products including swimwear, activewear, and outerwear.

PRESSURE: Continuous physical force on or against a surface by something in contact with it.

REFINE: Industrial process that converts oil into different useable products.

RESERVOIR: An underground rock formation containing oil confined by rock or water barriers.

TREAT: Also known as treating, is the process of removing unwanted contaminants and chemicals from the oil.